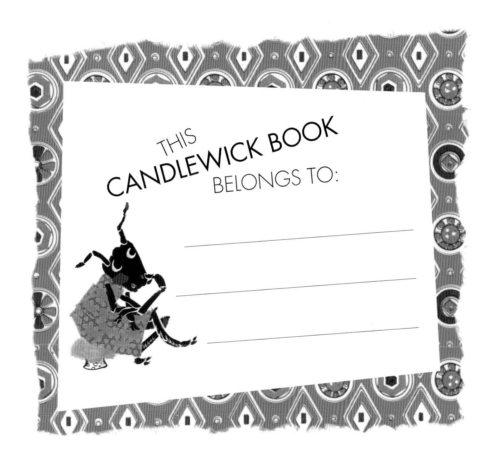

THIS
CANDLEWICK BOOK
BELONGS TO:

_____

_____

_____

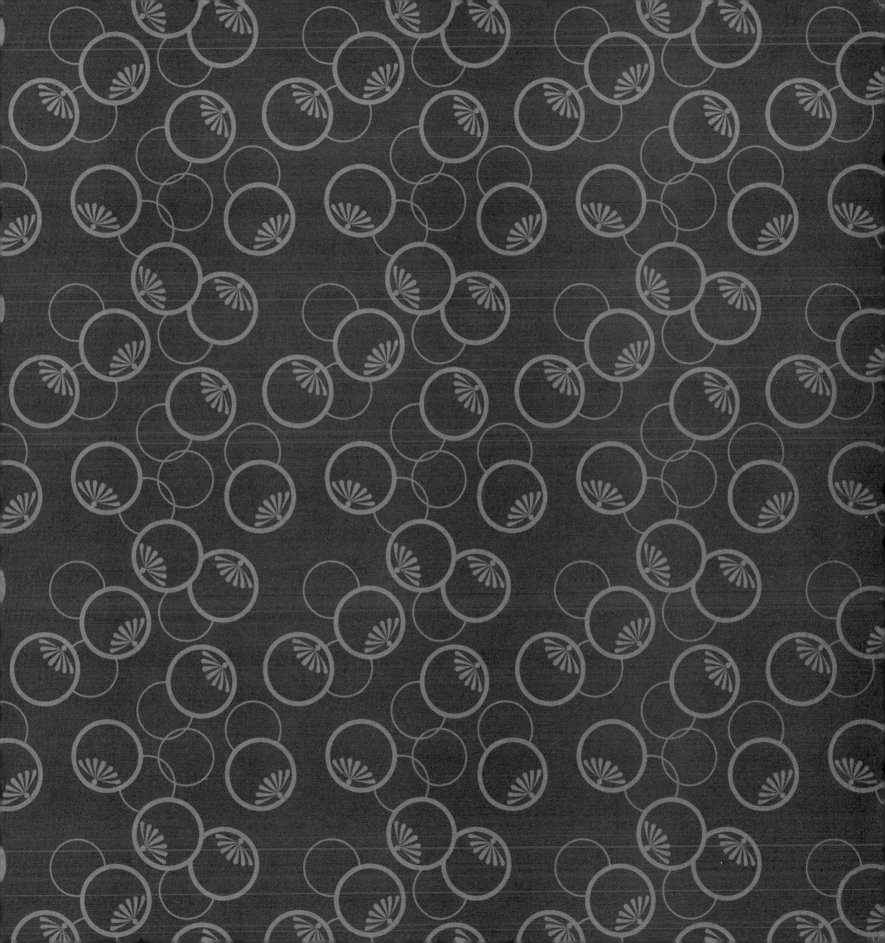

An
Everyday
Guide
to
Poetic Forms

SELECTED BY **PAUL B. JANECZKO**
ILLUSTRATED BY **CHRIS RASCHKA**

A KICK IN THE HEAD

PAUL B. JANECZKO

CHRIS RASCHKA

CANDLEWICK PRESS

For Kathy Leyden, who is everything a good teacher,
coach, and person should be
P. B. J.

For Jon
C. R.

Poems copyright © 2005 by Paul B. Janeczko · Illustrations copyright © 2005 by Chris Raschka

This collection copyright © 2005 by Paul B. Janeczko · Illustrations copyright © 2005 by Chris Raschka

All rights reserved. No part of this book may be reproduced, transmitted, or stored in an information retrieval system in any form or by any means, graphic, electronic, or mechanical, including photocopying, taping, and recording, without prior written permission from the publisher.

First paperback edition 2009

Library of Congress Cataloging-in-Publication Data
is available.

Library of Congress Catalog
Card Number 2004048508

ISBN 978-0-7636-0662-6 (hardcover)
ISBN 978-0-7636-4132-0 (paperback)

10 9 8 7 6 5 4 3 2 1

Printed in China

This book was typeset in Myriad.
The illustrations were done in watercolor, ink, and torn paper.

Candlewick Press
99 Dover Street
Somerville, Massachusetts 02144

visit us at www.candlewick.com

Contents

Introduction

Why, you may ask, do poems have rules? Why 17 syllables in a haiku? Why 14 lines in a sonnet? The answer is: rules make the writing of a poem more challenging, more exciting. Think of a game you enjoy, like baseball. Imagine how much less intriguing the game would be if there were no foul lines or no limit to the number of outs in an inning. The rules often ask, "Can you do a good job within these limits?" Knowing the rules makes poetry — like sports — more fun, for players and spectators alike. Robert Frost once remarked that poetry without rules would be like a tennis match without a net.

That said, in this book of 29 poetic forms, not all the examples strictly follow the rules of their form. Don't be shocked. Poets are sometimes more interested in following the spirit of a poetic form than being a slave to its every aspect. For example, when you read Steven Herrick's limerick on page 21, you'll notice immediately that he breaks the rules — and has fun doing so. Likewise, although the excerpt from Robert Service's ballad "The Shooting of Dan McGrew" follows the basic ballad rhyme scheme, it is not written in quatrains (stanzas, or verses, of four lines).

In a handful of explanations of the forms, I mention rhyme scheme and say something like, "The rhyme scheme in this stanza is *abba*." Using letters in this way tells the reader which lines rhyme. In my example *abba*, I am telling you that the first line rhymes with the fourth line, and the second line rhymes with the third.

Don't overlook the clever pictorial clues that Chris Raschka has included in the top corner of each page where a new poem is introduced. For example, the flowers on page 14 represent the 5-7-5 syllable count and arrangement of a haiku as well as its natural subject matter.

You can read this book any way you wish, of course, but let me offer a suggestion. Read a poem, then read the explanatory note at the bottom of the page. You'll find fuller explanations on pages 56–59. Then read the poem another time or two to see if you can tell how it follows — or departs from — the aspects of that particular poetic form. No matter how you read this book, though, be patient with the forms and enjoy the poems.

Enough from me. It's time to hear what the poets have to say.

—Paul B. Janeczko

Couplet

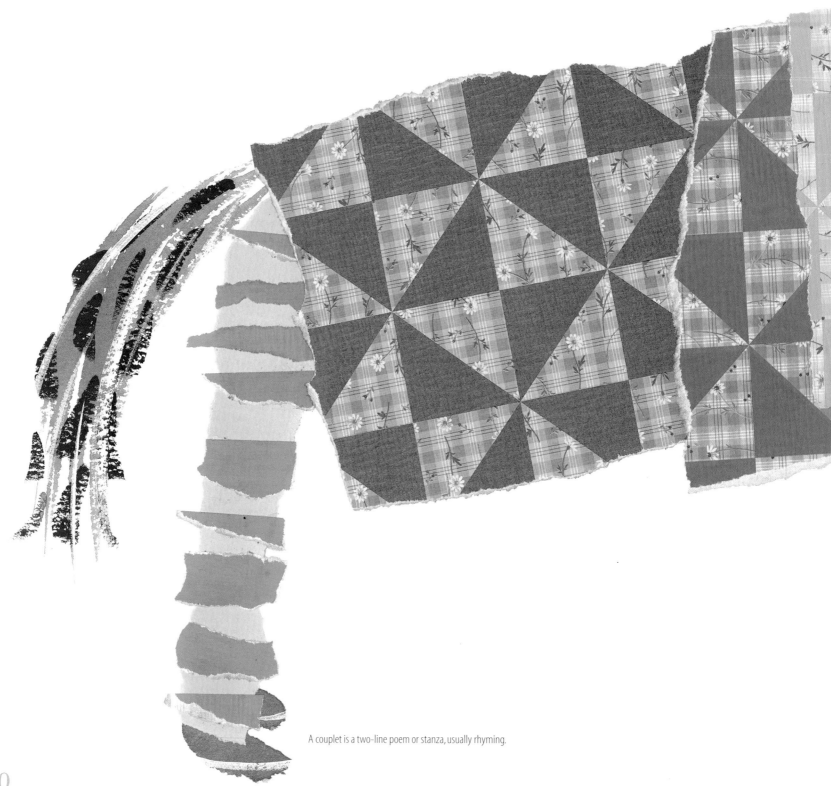

A couplet is a two-line poem or stanza, usually rhyming.

In the world of mules

There are no rules.

"The Mule" by Ogden Nash

Kitchen crickets make a din,

sending taunts to chilly kin,

"You're outside, but we got in."

Joan Bransfield Graham

If you have a couplet and add a third line with the same end rhyme, you wind up with a tercet (pronounced ter-SET or TER-sit).

Tyger Tyger, burning bright,

In the forests of the night;

What immortal hand or eye,

Could frame thy fearful symmetry?

"The Tyger" by William Blake

A quatrain is a four-line poem or stanza, usually rhymed *aabb* or *abab*.

Haiku

In the rains of spring,

An umbrella and raincoat

Pass by, conversing.

"Spring Rain" by Buson

A haiku contains three unrhymed lines and usually includes 17 syllables, arranged in lines of 5, 7, and 5 syllables. Haikus generally describe scenes in nature.

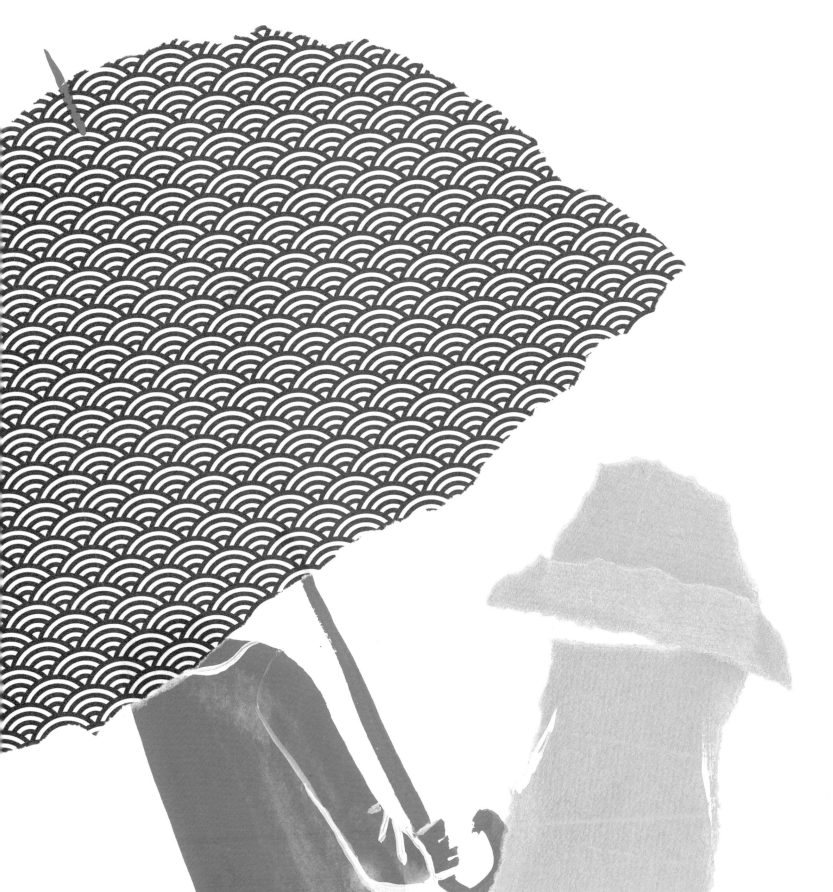

Senryu

First day, new school year,

backpack harbors a fossil . . .

last June's cheese sandwich.

Kristine O'Connell George

A senryu follows the same pattern as a haiku—three
lines of 5-7-5 syllables—but it is about human nature
rather than about the natural world around us.

16

Fish guts

stain the rowboat's planks;

by the lake's edge

a child is throwing stones

into the deep.

Penny Harter

The tanka is a five-line cousin of the haiku.
The accented syllables are usually counted: 2-3-2-3-3.

Cinquain

Oh, cat

are you grinning

curled in the window seat

as sun warms you this December

morning?

Paul B. Janeczko

The cinquain (SING-kane) is like the haiku in that it is composed of a set number of syllables (22) and a per-line syllable count (2-4-6-8-2).

Edgar Allan Poe

Was passionately fond of roe.

He always liked to chew some

When writing anything gruesome.

E. C. Bentley

A clerihew is made up of two
rhyming couplets that poke gentle
fun at a celebrity. The first line is
always the celebrity's name.

Limerick

There was an Old Lady whose folly

Induced her to sit in a holly;

    Whereupon, by a thorn

    Her dress being torn,

She quickly became melancholy.

Edward Lear

A limerick is a five-line poem with the rhyme scheme *aabba*. It has a bouncy rhythm and is usually humorous.

There once was a limerick called Steven

whose rhyme scheme was very uneven

it didn't make sense

it wasn't funny

and who'd call a limerick Steven anyway?

Steven Herrick

Roundel

A silver trapeze of my own: I dream of it nightly.

A slim silver bar at the end of a rope I seize

and am lifted, carried, I'm flying above the ground lightly.

A silver trapeze.

Down and around and up on the crest of a breeze

I swoop, I soar through a cloud, hesitate slightly,

then loop the loop like a pinwheel and hang from my knees.

Up through space I race on a bar shining brightly,

touch the tip of a star whenever I please,

kick off from the moon, sweep soundlessly down, holding tightly

a silver trapeze.

"A Silver Trapeze" by Alice Schertle

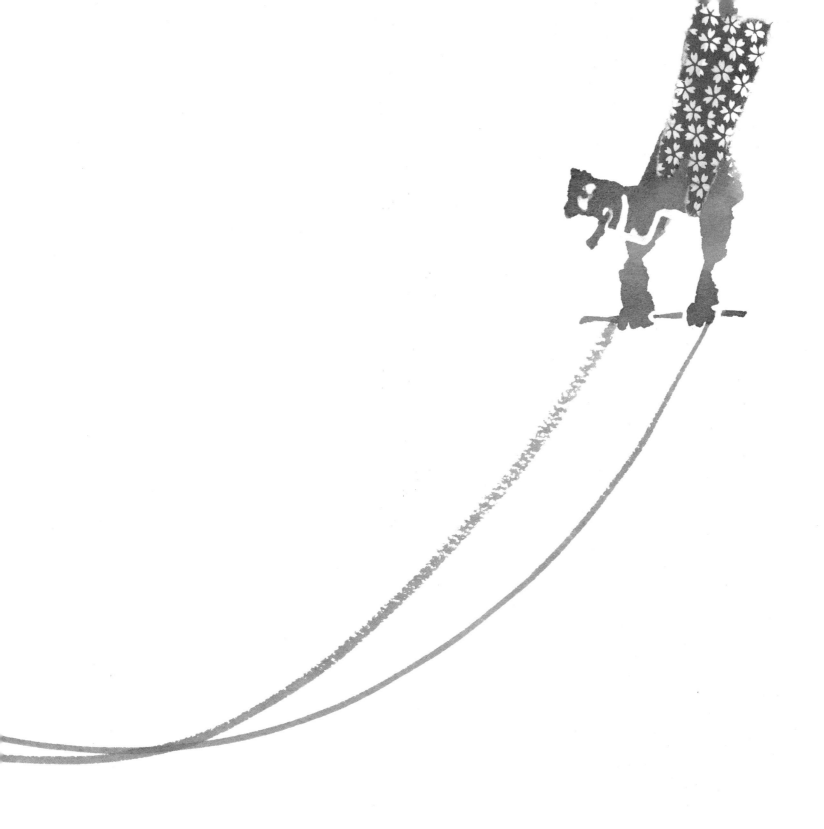

A roundel is a three-stanza poem of 11 lines. The stanzas have four, three, and four lines in them and a rhyme scheme of *abab bab abab*. Ah, but there's more. Line 4 is repeated as line 11 — not an easy trick!

Higgledy-Piggledy

William the Conqueror

Ousted King Harold in

Ten Sixty-Six,

Sacked Anglo-Saxons and,

Normanmaniacal,

Cut off their heads and dis-

Played them on sticks.

"History Lesson" by Allan Wolf

Higgledy, piggledy,

Benjamin Harrison,

Twenty-third President,

   Was, and, as such,

Served between Clevelands, and

Save for this trivial

Idiosyncrasy,

   Didn't do much.

**"Historical Reflections"
by John Hollander**

A dactyl is a three-syllable word or phrase in which the first syllable is accented and the other two aren't, such as *cereal*. A double dactyl is a humorous single-sentence poem spread over two quatrains, with two dactyls in most lines. Line 6 or 7 must be a one-word double dactyl, such as *antiheroically*.

Triolet

How unkind to keep me here

When, over there, the grass is greener.

Tender blades — so far, so near —

How unkind to keep me here!

Through this fence they make me peer

At sweeter stems; what could be meaner?

How unkind to keep me here

When, over there, the grass is greener.

"The Cow's Complaint" by Alice Schertle

A triolet is an eight-line poem in which line 1 repeats as lines 4 and 7 and line 2 repeats as line 8. The rhyme scheme is *abaaabab*.

Sonnet

When I do count the clock that tells the time,

And see the brave day sunk in hideous night;

When I behold the violet past prime,

And sable curls all silvered o'er with white:

When lofty trees I see barren of leaves,

Which erst from heat did canopy the herd,

And summer's green all girded up in sheaves

Borne on the bier with white and bristly beard:

Then of beauty do I question make,

That thou among the wastes of time must go,

Since sweets and beauties do themselves forsake,

And die as fast as they see others grow

  And nothing 'gainst time's scythe can make defence

  Save breed to brave him, when he takes thee hence.

"Sonnet Number Twelve" by William Shakespeare

When I do count the clock that tells the time

And see my whole day gone and all its light;

When I sort out this sonnet's classic rhyme

And try to comprehend with all my might;

When it occurs to me that I'll be teased

By fellow students after they have heard

My sonnet said upon these trembling knees

My fervent wish? That I'm disguised (with beard).

Then of *my* wisdom do I question make.

What was I thinking when I said I'd try

For Drama Club — was I not yet awake?

Now I must climb from this black hole hereby;

For nothing 'gainst Mr. J can make defense

Save bribes, to brave him when he hears me hence.

**"My Version of William Shakespeare's Sonnet Number Twelve"
by April Halprin Wayland**

There are two types of sonnets: Italian and Shakespearean. Both are 14 lines long and usually written in iambic pentameter, which means the lines are ten syllables, with an accent falling on every other syllable. The Shakespearean sonnet (as featured here) has a rhyme scheme of *abab cdcd efef gg*, which you will recognize as three quatrains and a couplet.

Villanelle

Is there a villain in your villanelle?

Just lurking, smirking in a line or two?

Read on, my dear, for only time will tell.

He'll try to show that you can't really spell.

Or hold a poem together without glue.

Is there a villain in your villanelle?

And what if you can't rhyme things very well?

Perhaps it is a plot by you-know-who.

Read on, my dear, for only time will tell.

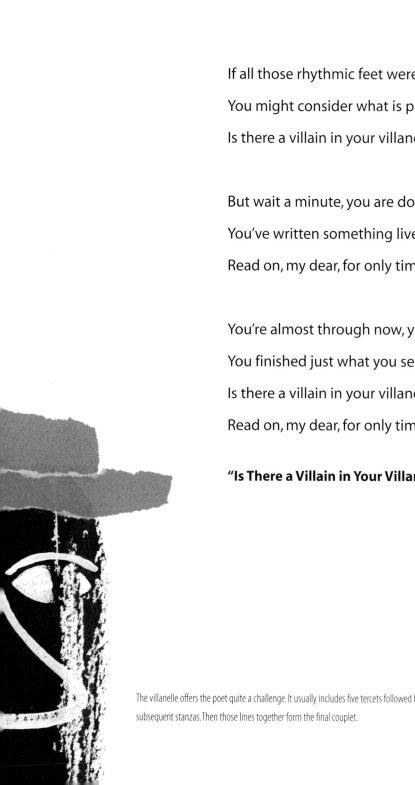

If all those rhythmic feet were tripped and fell,

You might consider what is plaguing you.

Is there a villain in your villanelle?

But wait a minute, you are doing swell.

You've written something lively, something new.

Read on, my dear, for only time will tell.

You're almost through now, you can give a yell.

You finished just what you set out to do.

Is there a villain in your villanelle?

Read on, my dear, for only time will tell.

"Is There a Villain in Your Villanelle?" by Joan Bransfield Graham

The villanelle offers the poet quite a challenge. It usually includes five tercets followed by a quatrain. Lines 1 and 3 take turns repeating as the third line of the subsequent stanzas. Then those lines together form the final couplet.

Opposites

What is the opposite of *two*?

A lonely me, a lonely you.

Richard Wilbur

This form plays with the idea of defining opposites.
It is written in couplets and is generally two to eight lines long.

The beginning of eternity

The end of time and space,

The beginning of every end,

The end of every place.

Anonymous

A riddle poem indirectly describes a person, place, thing, or idea. The reader must try to figure out the subject of the riddle. A riddle poem can be any length and usually has a rhyme scheme of *abcb* or *aabb*.

(the letter e)

They wait under Pablo's bed,

Rain-beaten, sun-beaten,

A scuff of green

At their tips

From when he fell

In the school yard.

He fell leaping for a football

That sailed his way.

But Pablo fell and got up,

Green on his shoes,

With the football

Out of reach.

Now it's night.

Pablo is in bed listening

To his mother laughing

To the Mexican *novelas* on TV.

His shoes, twin pets

That snuggle his toes,

Are under the bed.

He should have bathed,

But he didn't.

(Dirt rolls from his palm,

Blades of grass

Tumble from his hair.)

He wants to be

Like his shoes,

A little dirty

From the road,

A little worn

From racing to the drinking fountain

A hundred times in one day.

It takes water

To make him go,

And his shoes to get him

There. He loves his shoes,

Cloth like a sail,

Rubber like

A lifeboat on rough sea.

Pablo is tired,

Sinking into the mattress.

His eyes sting from

Grass and long words in books.

He needs eight hours

Of sleep

To cool his shoes,

The tongues hanging

Out, exhausted.

"Ode to Pablo's Tennis Shoes" by Gary Soto

An ode celebrates a person, animal, or object; it is often written without the constraints of formal structure or rhyme.

Acrostic

Can't

Avoid

Trouble

Paul B. Janeczko

36

Does

Only

Good

Anonymous

Acrostic poems are descriptive poems in which the first letter of each line spells out the subject of the poem.

Concrete Poem

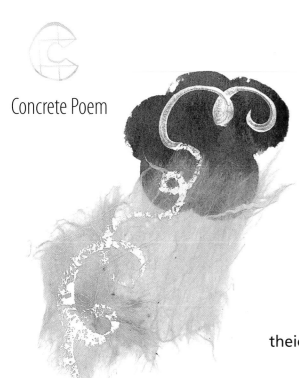

AmeliaCramped

inthe

cockpit

likeabirdinabox

theicecakedwings   theicecakedwings

shebringsjuice

toothbrush&comb

couragethewill

tofly15hrs.

without

stop

throughdarkdanger

the

Atlantic

sky

"Amelia Cramped" by Monica Kulling

The words in a concrete, or "shape," poem are arranged on the page to indicate the poem's subject.

```
                    poetry
                 jumpstarts
                 my imagin-
                     ation
                       it
opens its arms to me,  jabs me in the heart
                    thump
                    thump
                    poetry
                     gives
                      me
                       a

             k       p
             i         o
             c          e
             k           t
                          r
             i             y
             n
                     g
             t     i
             h       v
             e         e
                        s
             head          me a
```

```
                                    !
                                 K
                               C
                            I
                         K
```

"A Kick in the Head" by Joan Bransfield Graham

Epitaph

"Epitaph for Pinocchio" by J. Patrick Lewis

HERE
LIES.

Miss Spelling's

Exclamation points

Were myriad!!!

She lived on

The margin.

And died.

Period.

"Epitaph for a Book Editor" by J. Patrick Lewis

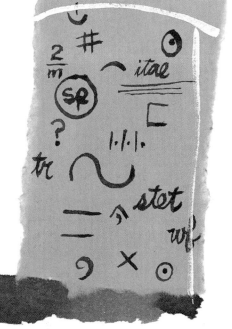

An epitaph is a short poem —— usually rhymed, often clever, with a play on words —— that draws on the tradition of verses that adorned tombstones in days of old.

Here lies resting, out of breath,

Out of turns, Elizabeth

Whose quicksilver toes not quite

Cleared the whirring edge of night.

Earth, whose circles round us skim

Till they catch the lightest limb,

Shelter now Elizabeth

And, for her sake, trip up death.

**"Little Elegy
(for a child who skipped rope)"
by X. J. Kennedy**

The elegy has no specific form but has a somber, sometimes mournful tone because it is generally about the death of an important or beloved person.

Found Poem

They fluttered from the sky like a sweet and peaceful snowstorm:

sheets and scraps — a crumpled page of cleaning instructions

with a reminder to damp-wipe smudges and smears;

a woman's cell-phone bill;

a hand-written note on paper decorated with kitchen herbs read:

". . . it would be nice to have another pot-luck dinner for parents";

a blank check numbered 3746 neatly torn from a check-book.

Bits of paper floated into the open classroom windows,

drifted into a second floor apartment window on Liberty Street.

At St. Paul's Cathedral, in Lower Manhattan,

three inches blanketed the old graves.

"The Paper Trail" by Georgia Heard

A found poem contains words or phrases not intended as poetry — perhaps a shopping list — and arranged on the page as a poem. "The Paper Trail" is an eloquent variation on the form.

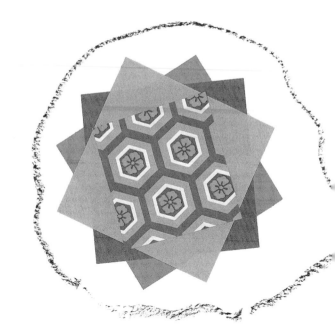

Neatly stacked in separate piles,

we wait

for the shape of a stencil —

the press of a pencil

the

snip   snip

snip

of silver scissors.

We wait

to become

lacy snowflakes

fat santas

pointy Christmas trees . . .

White, red, green —

now we are just paper.

We wait

quietly on a dark shelf,

dreaming

quietly

dreaming

of becoming . . .

"Paper Dreams" by Bobbi Katz

A persona poem is written from the point
of view of the poem's subject.

45

Poem of Address

You are him, from Maine,

him, from Montana,

and every him from sea

to sea and back.

Stewart, Kelly, York;

you are all of those

who shrimped on boats,

flew planes,

studied, wrote,

collected,

kissed.

The brave ones spill

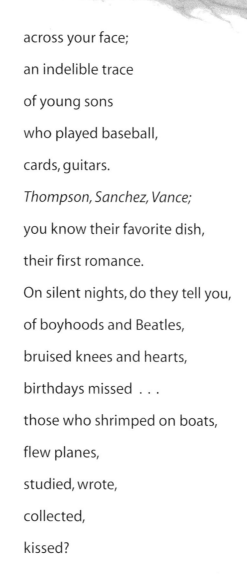

across your face;

an indelible trace

of young sons

who played baseball,

cards, guitars.

Thompson, Sanchez, Vance;

you know their favorite dish,

their first romance.

On silent nights, do they tell you,

of boyhoods and Beatles,

bruised knees and hearts,

birthdays missed . . .

those who shrimped on boats,

flew planes,

studied, wrote,

collected,

kissed?

"Whispers to the Wall"
(Vietnam Veterans Memorial, Washington, D.C. Dedicated 1982)
by Rebecca Kai Dotlich

In a poem of address, the poet writes as though speaking to a person or object.

Ballad

A bunch of the boys were whooping it up
      in the Malamute saloon;
The kid that handles the music-box
      was hitting a jag-time tune;
Back of the bar, in a solo game,
      sat the Dangerous Dan McGrew,
And watching his luck was his light-o'-love,
      the lady that's known as Lou.

When out of the night, which was fifty below,
      and into the din and the glare,

There stumbled a miner fresh from the creeks,

    dog-dirty, and loaded for bear.

He looked like a man with a foot in the grave

    and scarcely the strength of a louse,

Yet he tilted a poke of dust on the bar,

    and he called for drinks for the house.

There was none could place the stranger's face,

    though we searched ourselves for a clue;

But we drank his health, and the last to drink

    was the Dangerous Dan McGrew.

**Selection from "The Shooting of Dan McGrew"
by Robert W. Service**

Some ballads are written in couplets; others in six-line stanzas. A ballad tells a story, often coming from local history or legend and often involving lost love and tragedy.

Blues Poem

Just wiggling my toes

    in my brand new shoes.

Guess I've got a case

    of the back-to-school blues.

Shiny new notebook

    with nothing inside it.

Feeling kind of scared —

    trying to hide it.

What's waiting for me

    behind a classroom door?

A brand new teacher

    I've never seen before!

Maybe she's a good one.

    Maybe she's bad news.

I'm just a-wiggling,

    just a-jiggling —

got those back-to-school blues.

"Back-to-School Blues" by Bobbi Katz

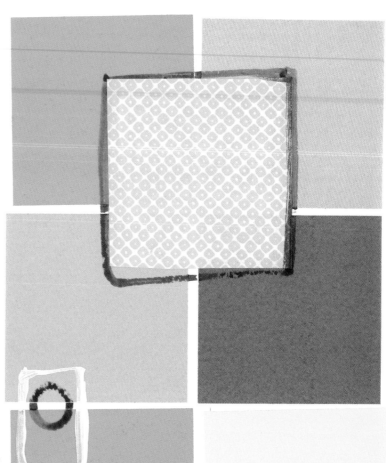

Original blues poems were written in three-line stanzas, but more and more of them are written in six-line stanzas. Some poets, like Bobbi Katz, have captured the plain-spoken, survivalist spirit of the blues without following a traditional form.

Home Address:

"Shady Lawn"

Working Hours:

dusk 'til dawn

Hobbies/Sports:

likes to climb

Special Skills:

making slime

Occupation:

midnight thief

Favorite Food:

salad leaf

Color Choice:

veggie green

Height and Weight:

long and lean

Next of Kin:

Mollusc clan

Appetite:

gargantuan

"Slug File" by Avis Harley

A list poem takes the deceptively simple everyday form of a list in order to describe something in detail. It can be rhymed or unrhymed.

Aubade

Morning has broken
Like the first morning,
Blackbird has spoken
Like the first bird.
Praise for the singing!
Praise for the morning!
Praise for them, springing
Fresh from the Word!

Sweet the rain's new fall
Sunlit from heaven,
Like the first dewfall
On the first grass.
Praise for the sweetness
Of the wet garden,
Sprung in completeness
Where his feet pass.

Mine is the sunlight!

Mine is the morning.

Born of the one light

Eden saw play!

Praise with elation.

Praise every morning,

God's re-creation

Of the new day!

Eleanor Farjeon

An aubade (oh-BAHD) laments or
celebrates the coming of the dawn.

Pantoum

Do I repeat myself?

There seems to be an echo in the room.

Oh, put the book back on the shelf!

And answer in the growing gloom.

There seems to be an echo in the room.

I see you turn to look at me

and answer in the growing gloom,

There isn't enough space for three!

I see you turn and look at me,

You say, It's just poetic form.

There isn't enough space for three

and yet another stanza just stuck out its arm.

You say it's just poetic form—

let's see how well *you* do!

And yet another stanza just stuck out its arm

and here I am at stanza four, and nearly through.

Hello? Hello! Hello, pantoum, hello!

Oh, put that book back on the shelf!

The book of forms, that ghastly book, oh, no —

Do I I I . . . repeat, repeat myself?

"Haunted Poem Pantoum" by Liz Rosenberg

A pantoum is an interlocking series of quatrains, with lines 2 and 4 of each stanza repeated as lines 1 and 3 of the next stanza. The final stanza adds a finishing touch — as lines 2 and 4 repeat lines 3 and 1 of the *opening* stanza. Whew!

55

Notes on the Forms

Couplet

A *couple* is two things that go together, as in "They're such a nice couple." A *couplet* is two lines of *poetry* that go together, usually rhyming and usually expressing a complete thought. A couplet can stand alone, as in Ogden Nash's many humorous examples; it can also act as a building block for other forms.

Tercet

If you have a couplet and add a third line with the same end rhyme, you wind up with a tercet. Some people call this poetic form a *triplet*.

Quatrain

The quatrain, the most common stanza in English poetry, is made up of four lines. Although it can be unrhymed, poets usually follow an *abab* or *abba* rhyme scheme. You'll see this form in action in the sonnet and the pantoum.

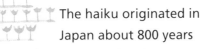

Haiku

The haiku originated in Japan about 800 years ago. Each poem contains three unrhymed lines and usually includes 17 syllables, arranged in lines of 5, 7, and 5 syllables. A haiku usually describes a scene in nature and includes a seasonal reference.

Senryu

I like to call senryu "haiku with an attitude." A senryu follows the same pattern as a haiku—three lines of 5-7-5 syllables— but it is about human nature rather than the natural world around us.

Tanka

The tanka is a five-line cousin of the haiku and has been a popular form of poetry in Japan for more than 1,300 years. Rather than count the total number of syllables in the poem, some tanka poets prefer to hear the accented syllables in each line: 2-3-2-3-3. And unlike the haiku, the tanka can include figures of speech such as metaphors and similes.

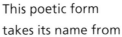

Cinquain

This poetic form takes its name from the Latin word *quinque,* "five." The cinquain is like the haiku in that it is composed of a set number of syllables (22) and a per-line syllable count (2-4-6-8-2). A good cinquain will flow from beginning to end rather than sounding like five separate lines.

Clerihew

Like many of the poetic forms included in this book, the clerihew has a set number of lines: four. Specifically, the clerihew is made up of two couplets. And those couplets poke gentle fun at a celebrity. Perhaps the most challenging part of the clerihew is that the second line must rhyme with the first line, which is always the celebrity's name.

Limerick

The limerick is one of the most widely recognized poetic forms in the English language. It's a five-line poem that is made up of three lines (1, 2, and 5) with three accented syllables and two shorter lines (3 and 4) with two accented syllables. Read a good limerick out loud and you'll hear its rhythm bouncing along.

Roundel

Writing a roundel is a lot like putting together a jigsaw puzzle: you need to get all the pieces in place to see the whole picture. A roundel is a three-stanza poem with a total of 11 lines. The stanzas have four, three, and four lines in them and a rhyme scheme of *abab bab abab*. Ah, but there's more. Lines 4 and 11 use the same line or phrase, and the end words of those lines rhyme with lines 2, 5, 7, 9. Got it?

Double Dactyl

No, a double dactyl is not some sort of two-headed dinosaur. A dactyl is a three-syllable word or phrase in which the first syllable is accented and the other two are not, such as *interstate* or *cereal*. A double dactyl is a humorous one-sentence poem spread over two quatrains, with two dactyls in most lines. But wait! There's more: Lines 4 and 8 consist of just one dactyl, along with an extra accented syllable, and they rhyme. Line 6 or 7 is a one-word double dactyl, like *antiheroically*. Put it all together and—higgledy-piggledy—you've got a double dactyl!

Triolet

Although you might expect a triolet to have three lines, it actually has eight. The triolet gets its name from the fact that the first line occurs three times within the poem. In fact, the first two lines of the poem repeat as the last two lines of the poem and the opening line is also repeated as line 4. The rhyme scheme of a triolet looks like this: *abaaabab*.

Sonnet

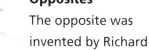

One of the most revered poetic forms in the English language, the sonnet originated in Italy in the thirteenth century. It started showing up in English around 1530. So it is that we have two types of sonnets: Italian and Shakespearean. Both are 14 lines long. Both are generally written in iambic pentameter, which means the lines contain ten syllables, with a stress falling on every other syllable, as in "Until you try our pie, you'll not know pie." The Shakespearean sonnet has a rhyme scheme of *abab cdcd efef gg*, which you will recognize as three quatrains and a couplet. The Italian sonnet has this rhyme scheme: *abba cddc efg efg*.

Villanelle

The villanelle offers the poet quite a challenge. It usually includes five tercets followed by a quatrain. The rhyme scheme is *aba* for the tercets and *abaa* for the quatrain. Now things get interesting. Lines 1 and 3 of the opening stanza are repeated alternately as the third lines of the rest of the tercets. Together, those two lines form the final couplet in the final stanza.

Opposites

The opposite was invented by Richard Wilbur when he published a book called (what else?) *Opposites,* about 40 years ago. An opposite can be as long as a poet wants it to be, but it must be written in couplets. Some opposites start with the question "What is the opposite of _____?" and answer that question in the rest of the poem. Others simply begin with "The opposite of _____" and complete that statement in the poem.

Riddle Poem

Riddle poems may have been around for hundreds of years in the literature of many cultures. The object of this poetic form is to indirectly describe a person, place, thing, or idea, and see if the reader can figure out the subject of the riddle. A good riddle poem, therefore, should be puzzling but not impossible. That's no fun. A riddle poem usually rhymes, most often in the scheme *abcb* or *aabb*.

Ode

An ode is a poem of celebration. Early odes, like those written in ancient Greece, were quite formal. Over time, however, many poets have come to realize that they can write an ode without the constraints of formal structure. So contemporary odes follow no rhyme scheme or stanza pattern. But they do celebrate!

Acrostic

Acrostic poems are great fun to write. They are basically descriptive poems that can be as long as the poet wants to make them. There's a catch, however. When read downward, the first letter of each line must form a word or phrase, usually the subject of the poem.

Concrete Poem

Some people call concrete poems "shape poems," which strikes me as a more accurate description because the words in the poem are arranged on the page to show the shape of the subject of the poem. In this way, a concrete poem is more purely visual than a traditional poem. The poem on page 38 is about the aviator Amelia Earhart.

Epitaph

An epitaph is a short poem—usually rhymed to some degree, often clever, with a play on words—that draws on the tradition of verses that adorned tombstones in days of old. Both traditional and modern epitaph poems are brief and act as tributes to the deceased person, usually making a comment on their personality or the way in which they lived.

Elegy

The elegy is another poetic form that goes back to the ancient Greeks. Like the modern ode and aubade, elegies have no specific form but they have a somber, sometimes mournful tone about them because they are usually about the death of an important or much-loved person. Walt Whitman wrote "When Lilacs Last in the Dooryard Bloomed" because he was moved by the death of Abraham Lincoln. Some elegies, such as Thomas Gray's "Elegy (Written in a Country Churchyard)," are more general laments about the passing of time.

Found Poem

Some people will tell you that a found poem is not really a poem. Nevertheless, found poems are worth exploring for their poetic content. A found poem is a piece of writing that wasn't intended as poetry. In other words, it's up to the poet to find poetic words and phrases in a prose piece—like a newspaper article or an outdoor gear catalog—and declare them a poem, often by arranging the words and phrases on the page. Georgia Heard's poem is not, strictly speaking, a completely found poem, since it includes some of her own words, but it's an eloquent variation on the form, touching on the theme of finding poetry in tragedy. (The scraps of paper she describes fell from the World Trade Center towers on September 11, 2001.)

Persona Poem

A persona poem is written from the point of view of the subject of the poem. For example, what might your pet parrot say if it could speak? Or that stuffed elephant your little sister drags everywhere she goes? Some people call this type of poem a mask poem because the poet is, in a sense, wearing a mask of the subject of the poem. Think about how you put on a mask at Halloween and become somebody or something different, and you get the idea of a persona poem.

Poem of Address

A poem of address is, roughly speaking, the flip side of a persona poem. Rather than using his or her imagination to write what an object is saying or thinking, in a poem of address the poet writes as though speaking to a person or an object. The poem is not *about* the object—although we will likely learn about it in the poem—but *to* the object.

Ballad

The ballad was originally an oral form of poetry. Traditional ballads were written in quatrains with a rhyme scheme of *abcb*. Lines 1 and 3 have four accented syllables or beats, while the rhyming lines have three beats. Some ballads are written in couplets and others are written in six-line stanzas. A ballad tells a story, often coming from local history or legend and often involving lost love and tragedy.

Blues Poem

The blues poem (a blues song without the music) has its roots in Africa, but the blues have been around in America since before the Civil War. As they worked in the fields, Southern slaves sang "field hollers," a sort of singing talk. Original blues songs were three-line stanzas, but more and more of them are written as six-line stanzas, the longer lines divided into two shorter lines. Some poets, like Bobbi Katz, capture the survivalist spirit of the blues without following a traditional form.

List Poem

A list poem is great fun to write because the poet gets to include lots of rich details about a subject. You might write a list poem about your friends—give a few memorable details about each—or about a family vacation, maybe with details of how things went wrong. A list poem is more than a list: it uses details and precise language to show the reader what the poet has noticed about a thing or situation.

Aubade

In Act 3, Scene 5 of *Romeo and Juliet*, the young lovers speak some of the most poignant words of the play as they lament the coming of the dawn that will separate them. This sense of lament for the coming of the new day is often the subject of an aubade. Other aubades celebrate the coming of the dawn. Like the *ode*, the aubade requires no formal structure or rhyme scheme, though some may have both.

Pantoum

A pantoum follows a complicated formula. It is written in quatrains and can be of any length. If the lines in the quatrains rhyme, the rhyme scheme is usually *abab*. So far so good, but here comes the tricky part. Lines 2 and 4 of each stanza are repeated as lines 1 and 3 of the next stanza, and this pattern is followed for the rest of the poem, regardless of how long it is. But hold on! There's one more noteworthy thing about a pantoum: in the final stanza, lines 1 and 3 are lines 2 and 4 of the previous stanza **and** lines 2 and 4 are lines 3 and 1 of the *opening* stanza. When all is said and done, every line in a pantoum is used twice, and the final line is the same as the first line.

Acknowledgments

"The Mule" by Ogden Nash. Copyright 1950 by Ogden Nash. Reprinted by permission of Curtis Brown Ltd.

"Kitchen crickets make a din,""Is There a Villain in Your Villanelle?," and "A Kick in the Head" by Joan Bransfield Graham. Copyright © 2005 by Joan Bransfield Graham. Reprinted by permission of the author.

"First day, new school year" by Kristine O'Connell George. Reprinted by permission of the author.

"Fish guts" by Penny Harter. Reprinted by permission of the author.

"Oh, cat" and "Cat" by Paul B. Janeczko. Reprinted by permission of the author.

"There once was a limerick called Steven" by Steven Herrick, from *My Life, My Love, My Lasagne* by Steven Herrick, University of Queensland Press, 1997.

"A Silver Trapeze" by Alice Schertle. Reprinted by permission of the author.

"History Lesson" by Allan Wolf. Reprinted by permission of the author.

"Historical Reflections" by John Hollander, from *Jiggery-Pokery: A Compendium of Double Dactyls* by Anthony E. Hecht and John Hollander. Copyright © 1966 by Anthony E. Hecht and John Hollander. Reprinted by permission of Scribner, an imprint of Simon & Schuster Adult Publishing Group.

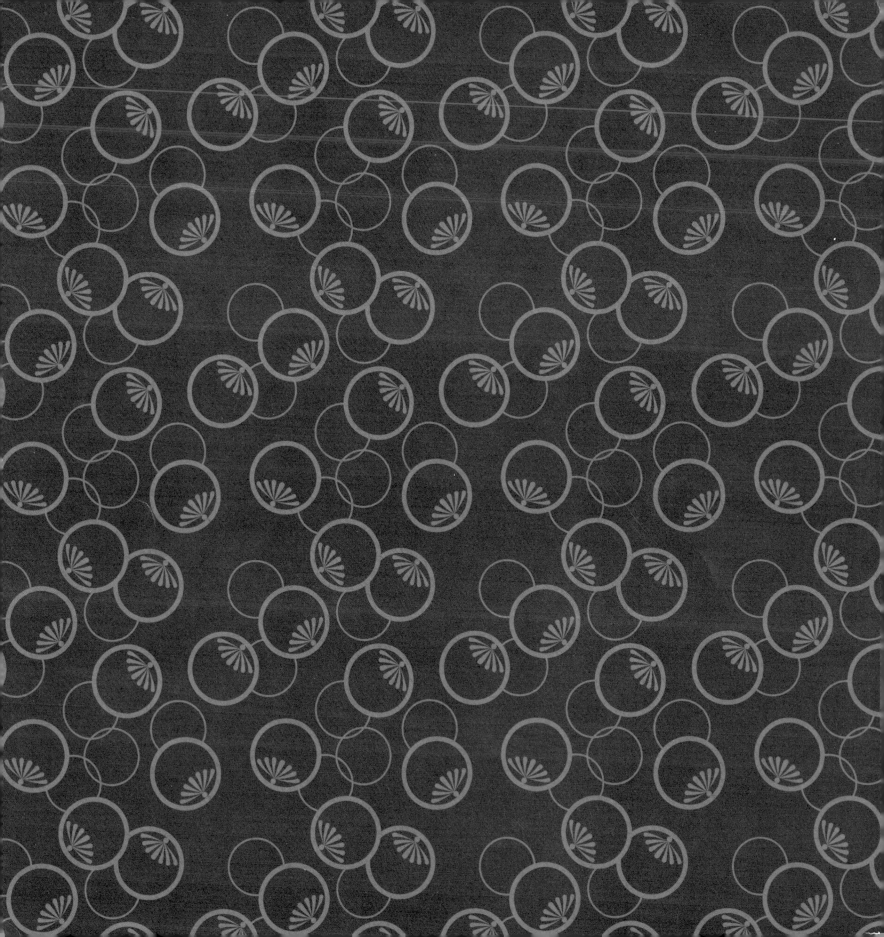